I0467613

How To Draw Realistic Skulls Volume 1

Simple Guide to Drawing Skulls

How to Draw Skulls

By : Gala Publication

Published By :

Gala Publication

© Copyright 2015 – Gala Publication

ISBN-13: **978-1522785606**
ISBN-10: **1522785604**

Table of Contents

4

CHOLO SKULL

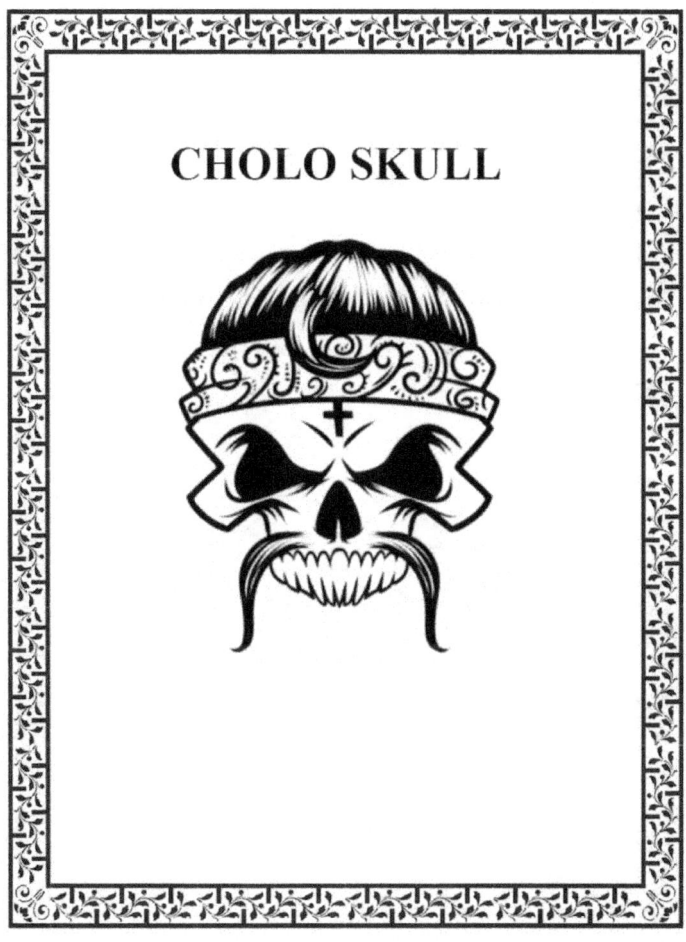

STEP 1

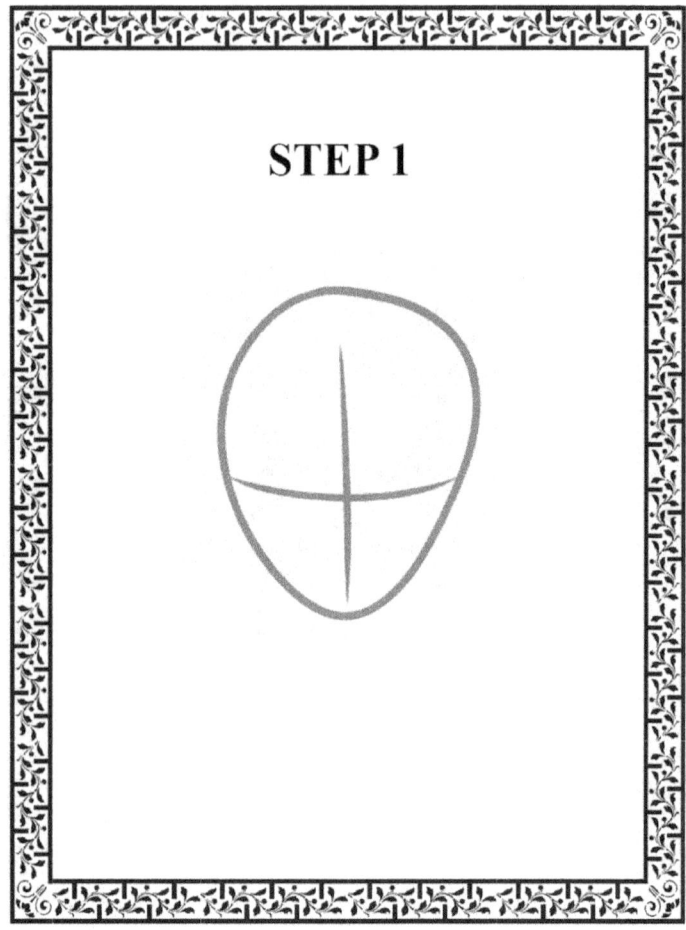

STEP 2

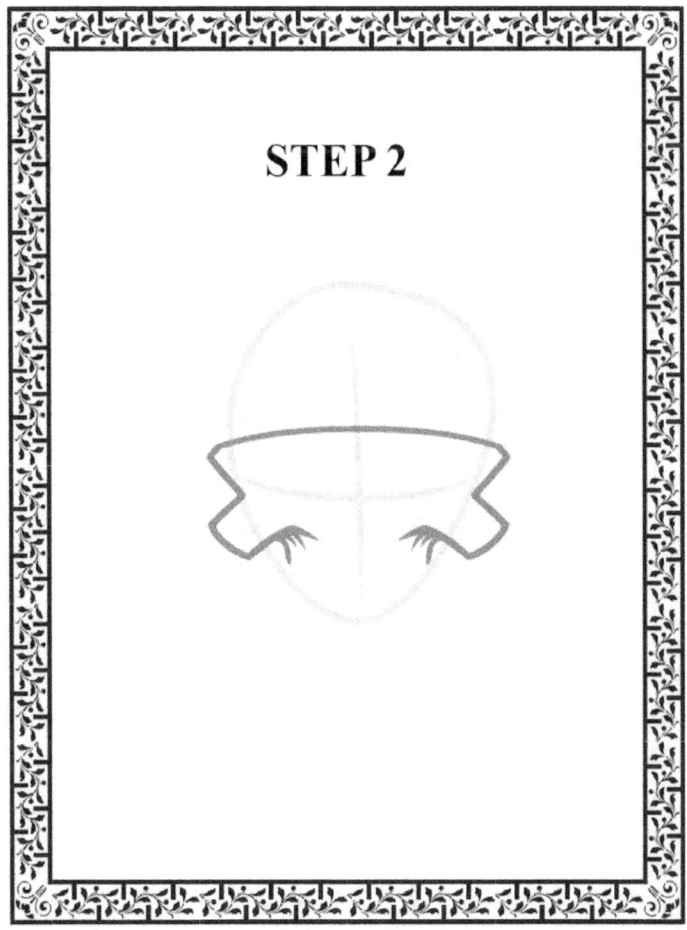

STEP 3

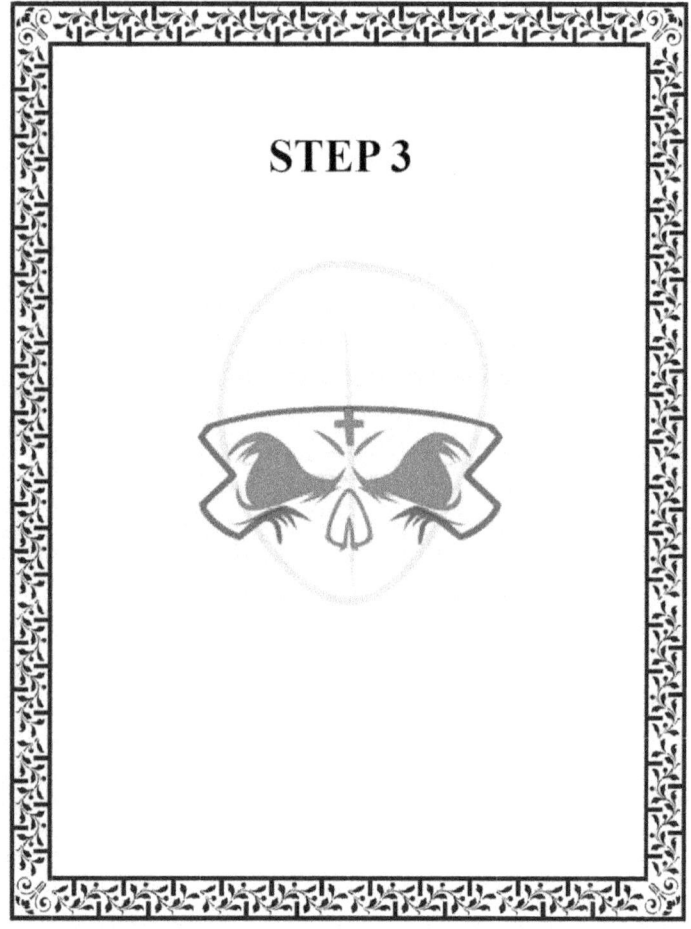

STEP 4

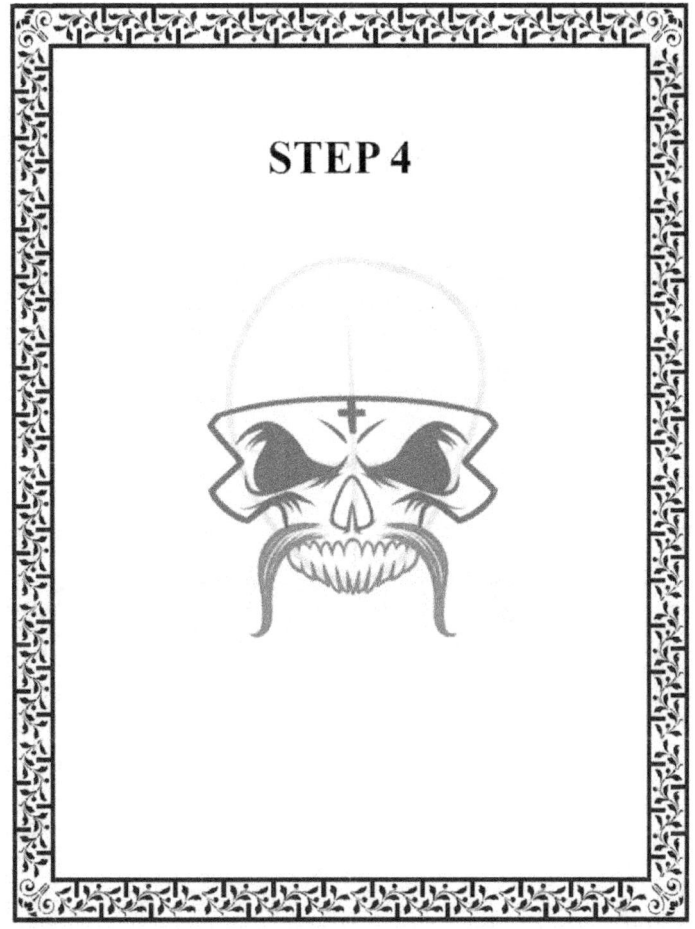

STEP 5

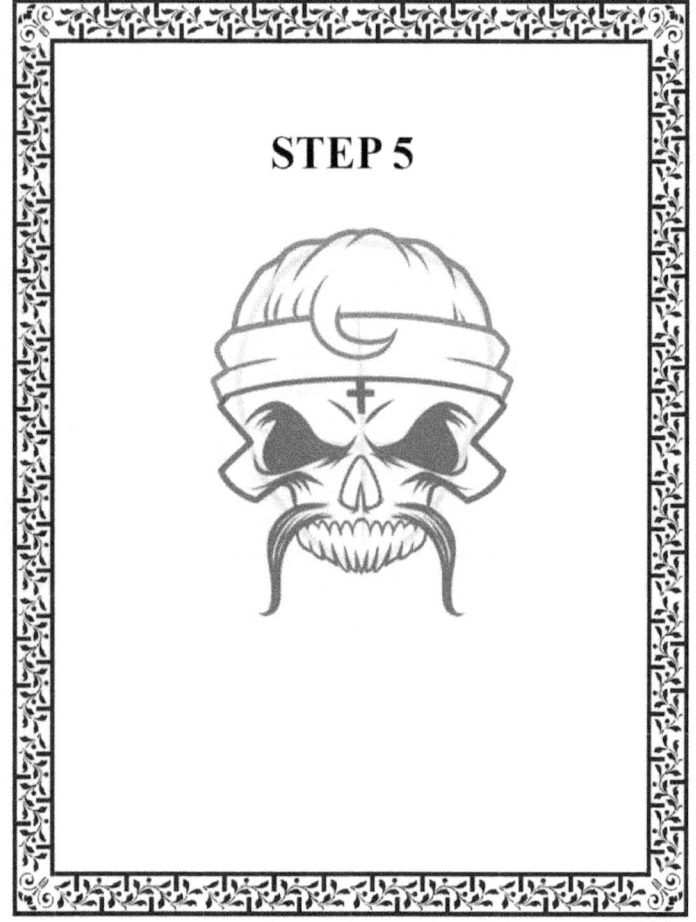

STEP 6

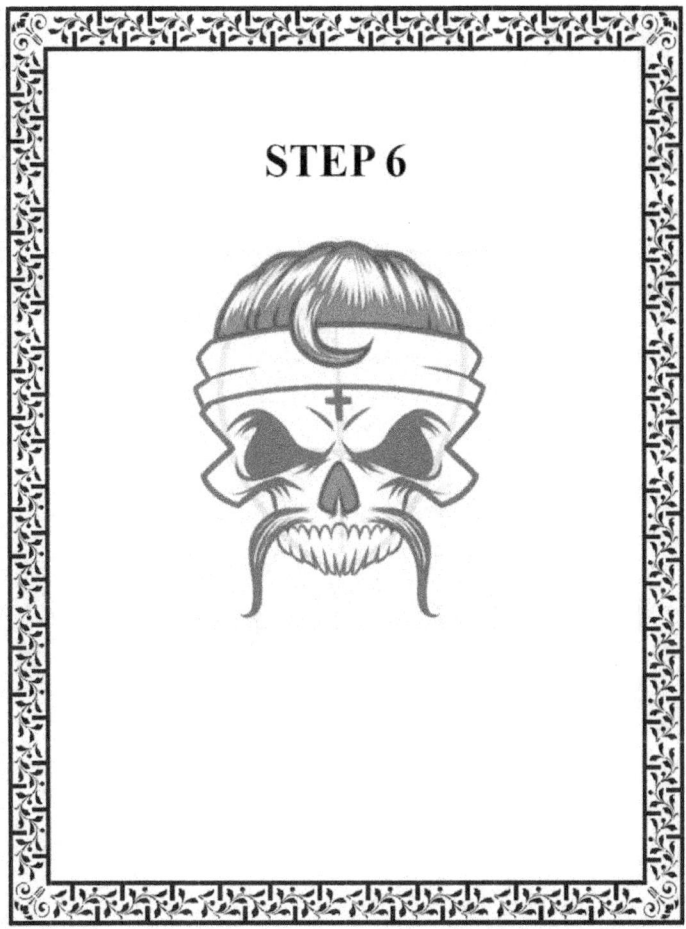

STEP 7

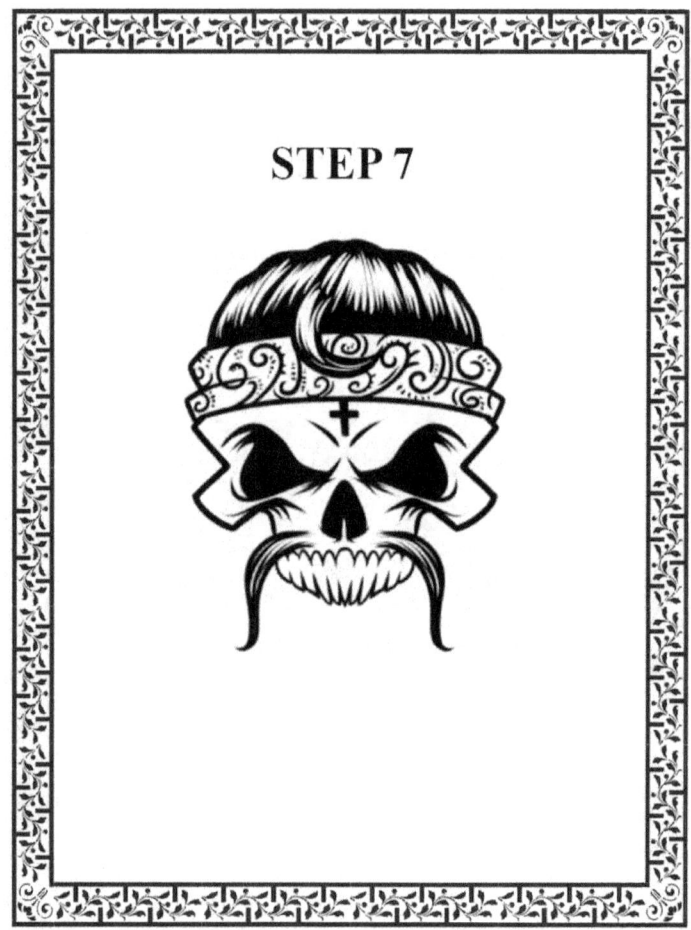

13

CHROME SKULL

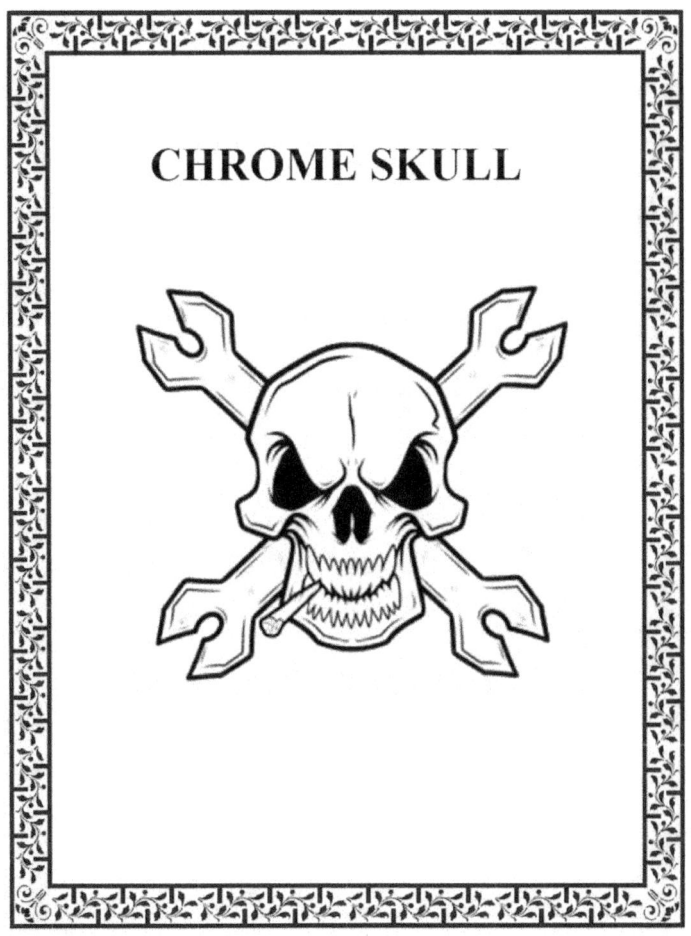

STEP 1

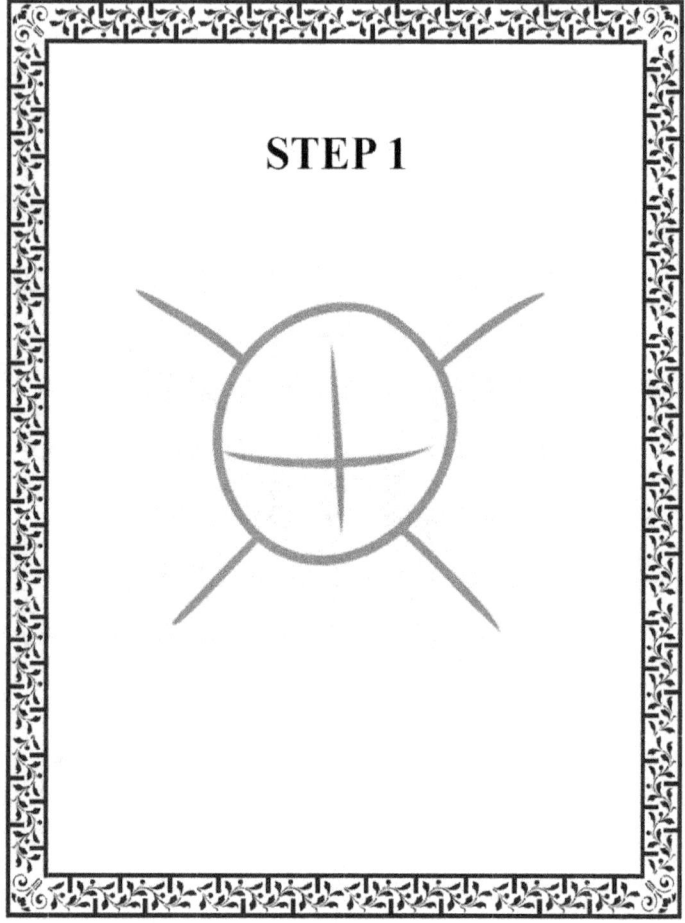

STEP 2

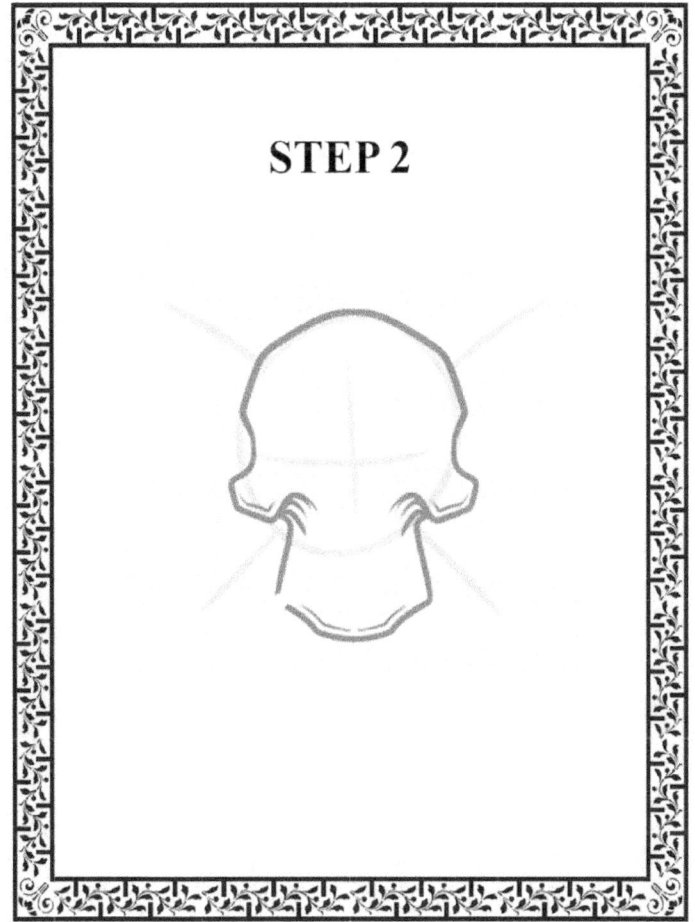

STEP 3

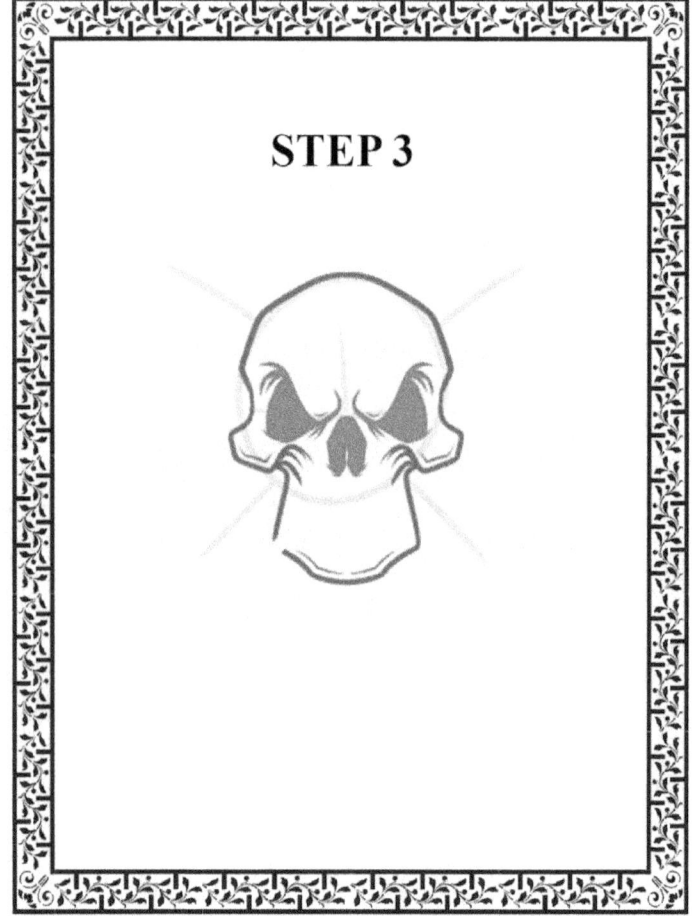

STEP 4

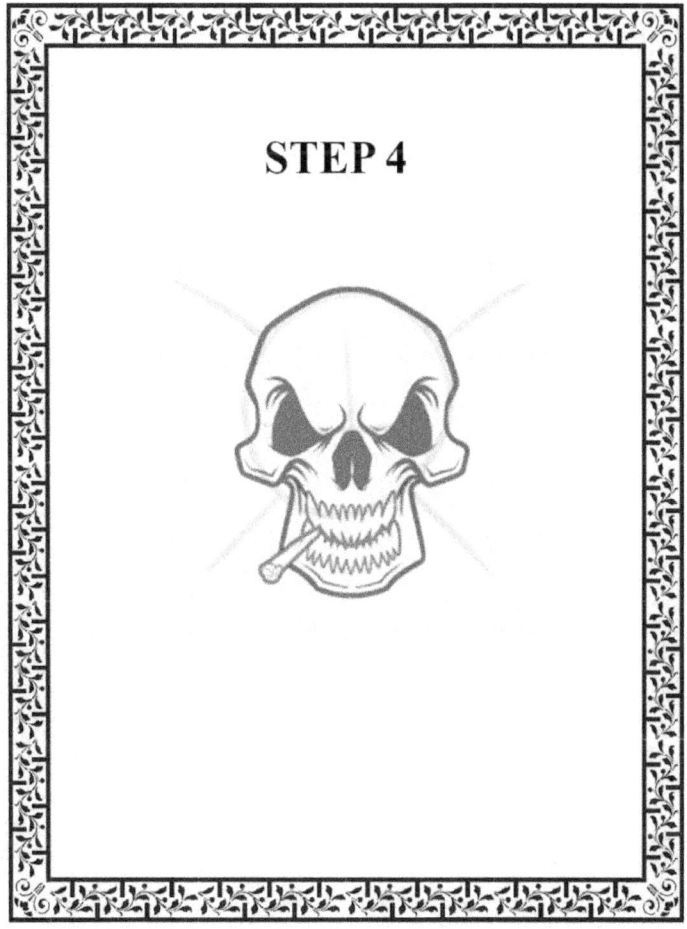

STEP 5

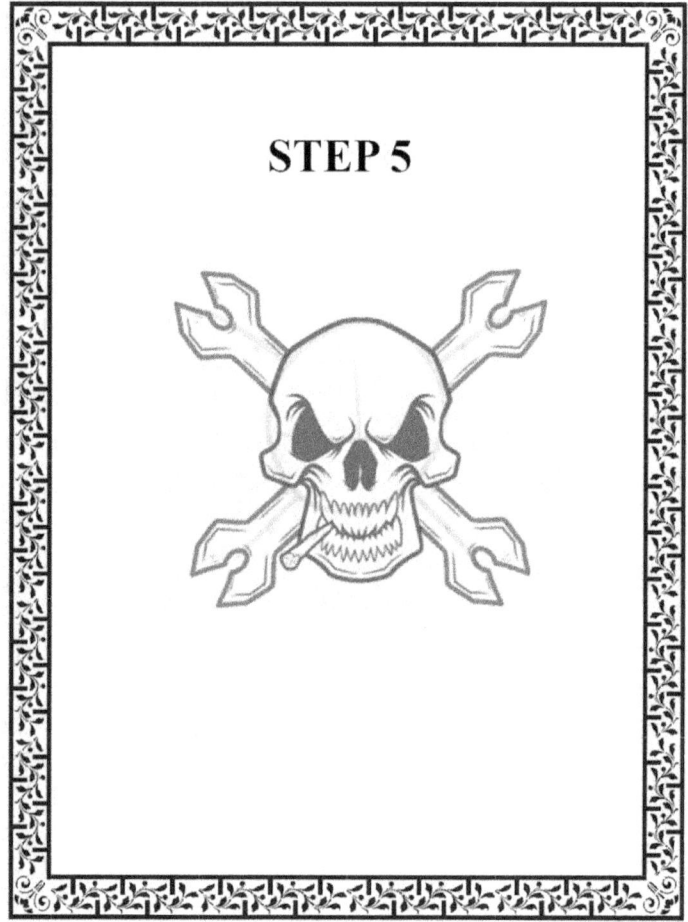

STEP 6

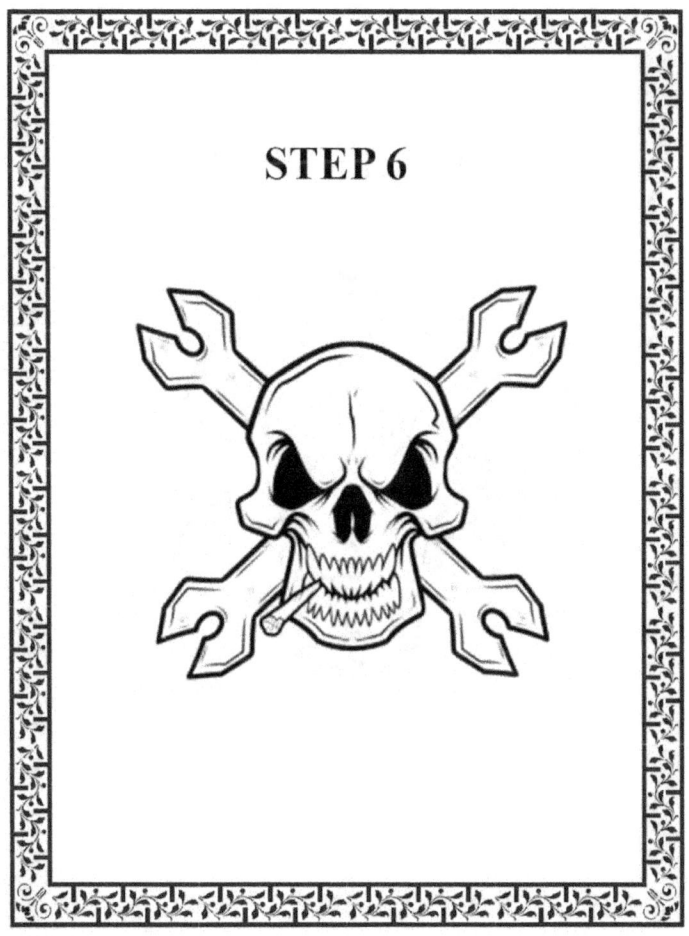

EMOJI SKULL

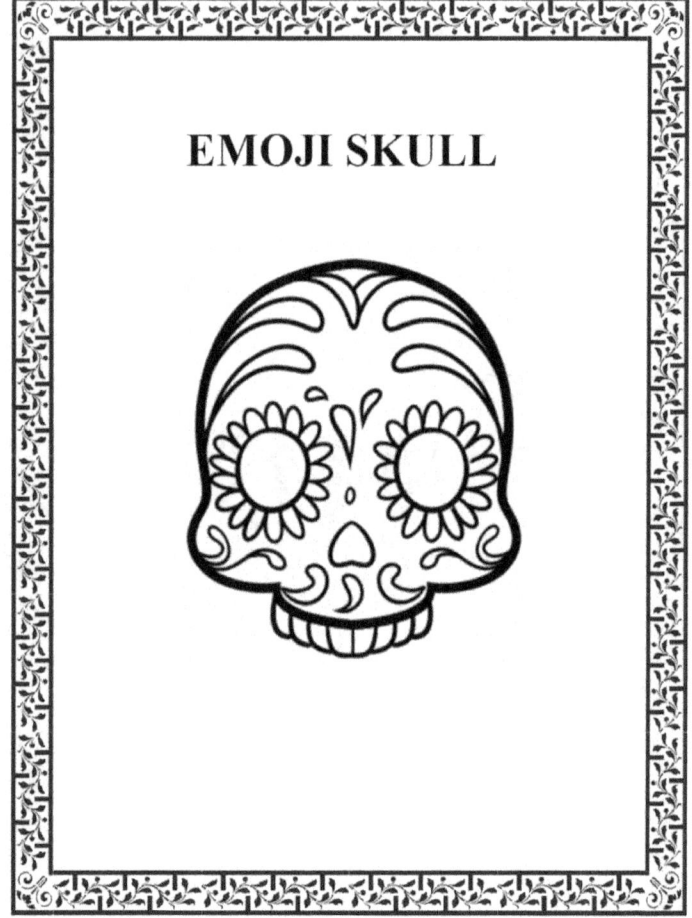

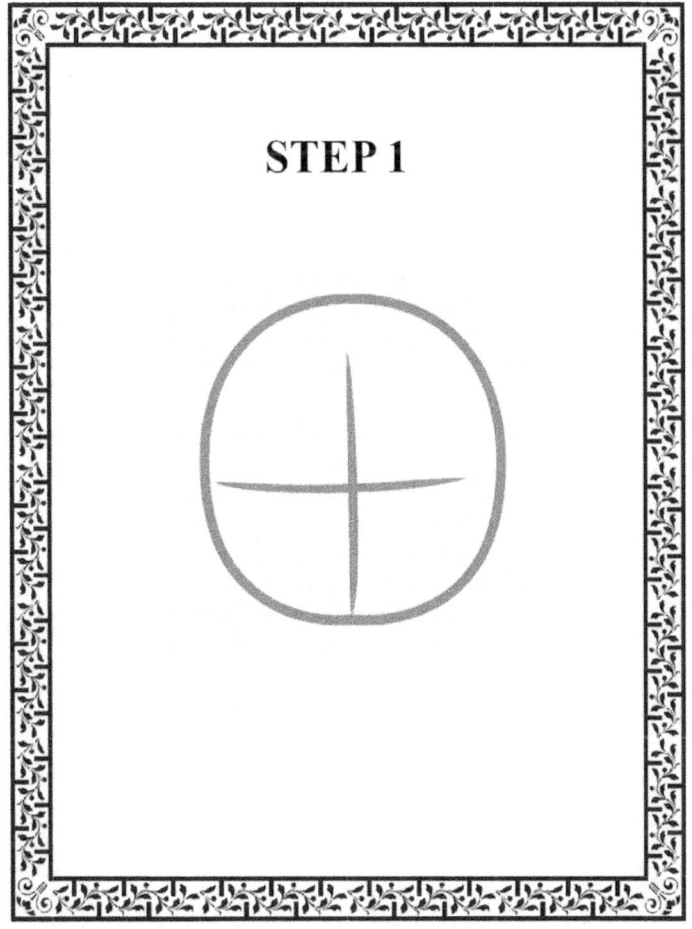

STEP 1

STEP 2

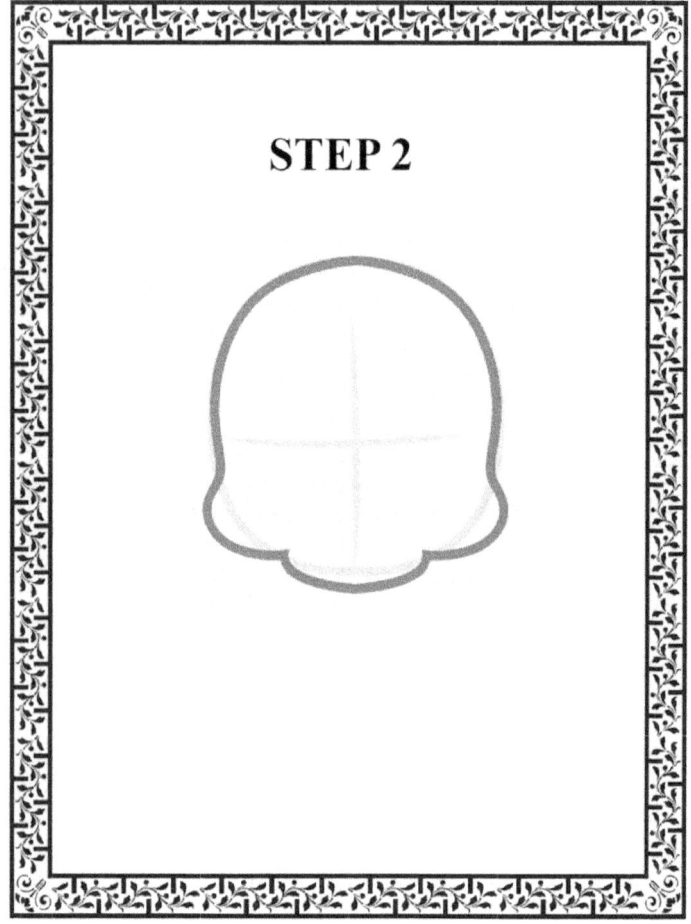

STEP 3

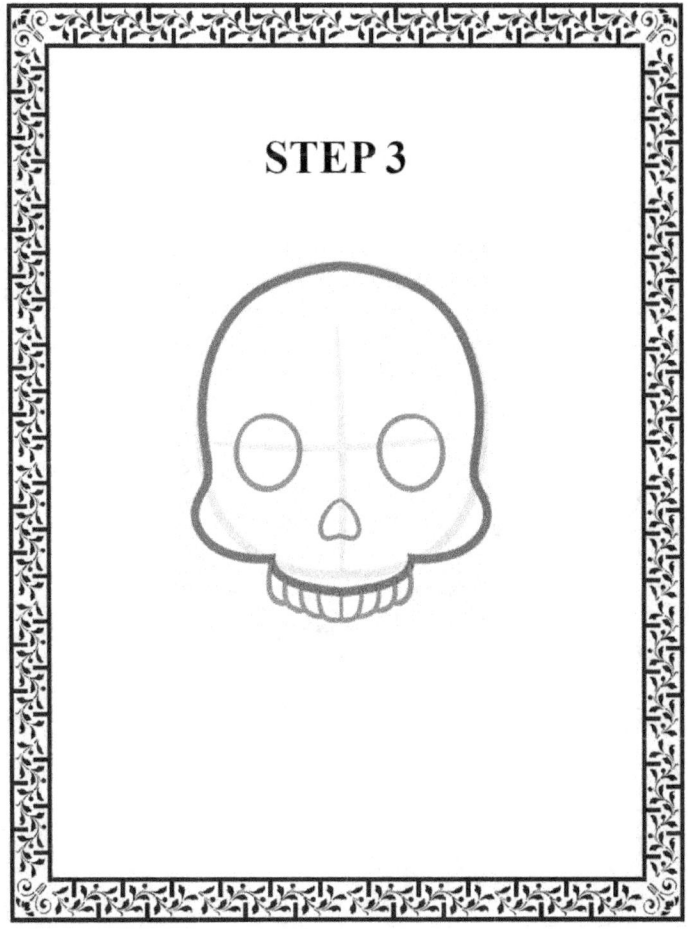

STEP 4

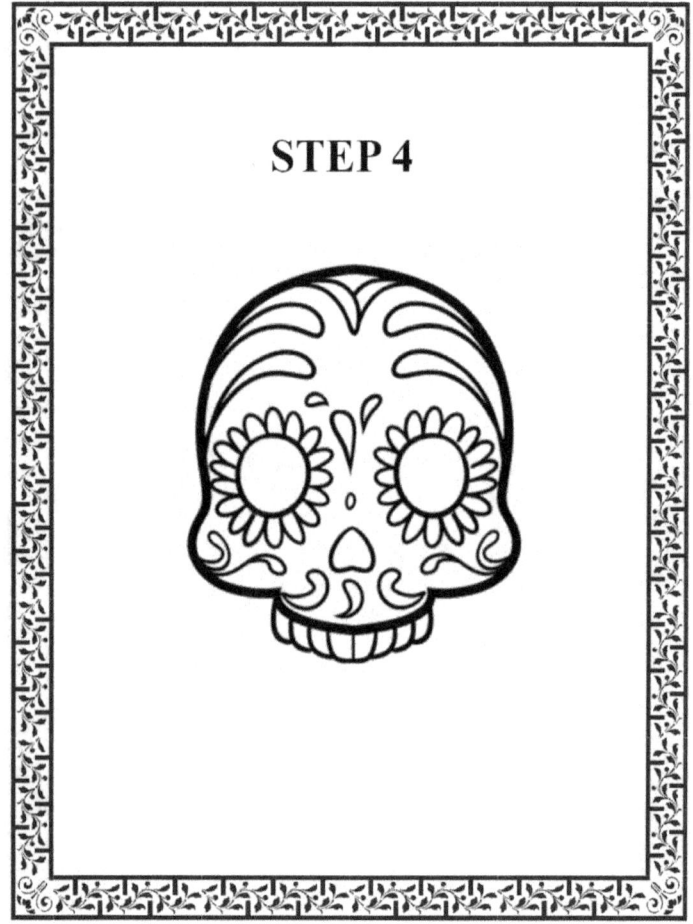

IRON CROSS SKULL

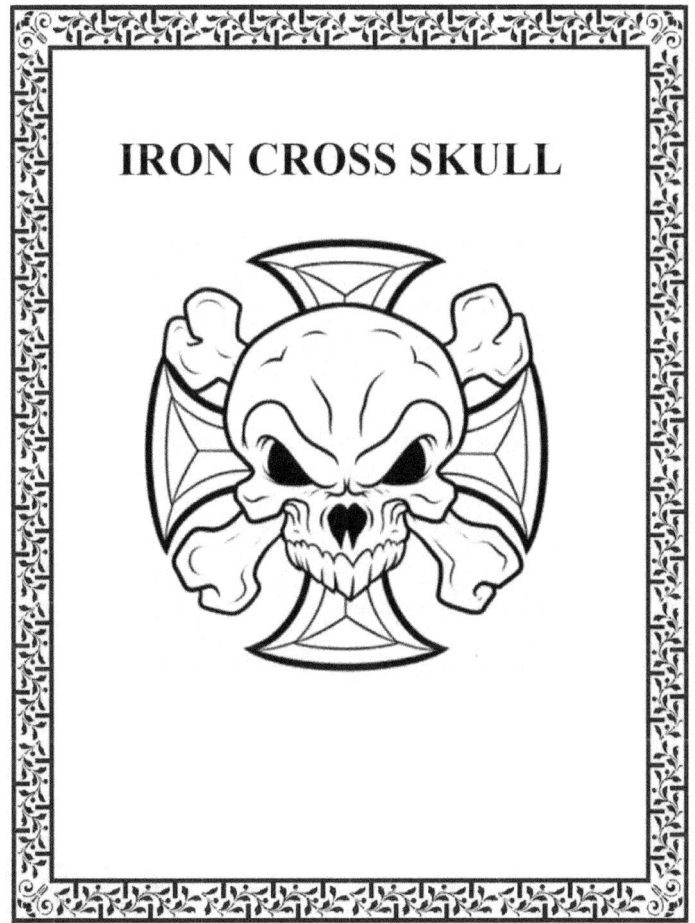

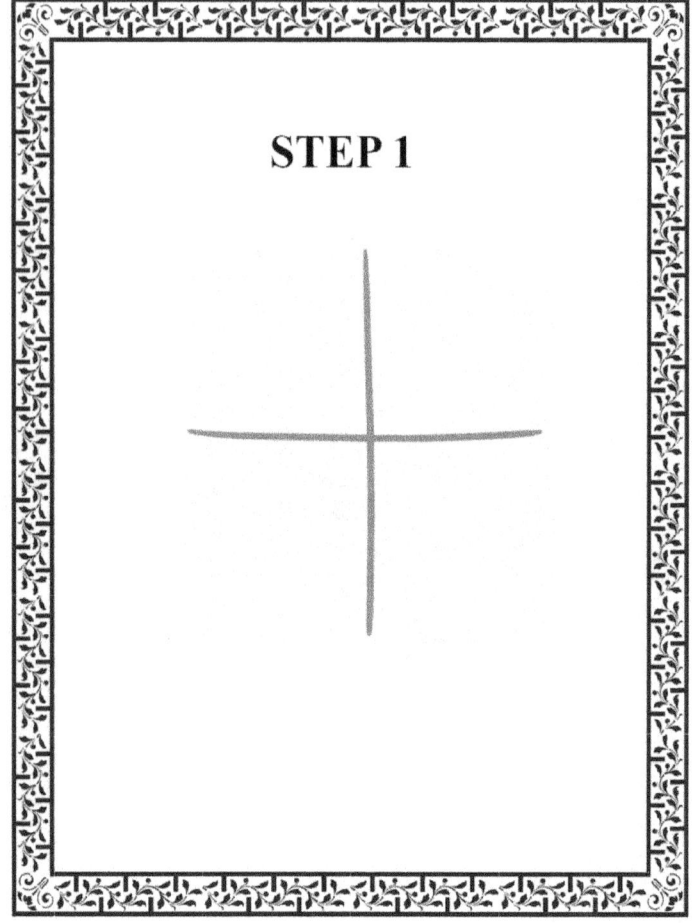

STEP 2

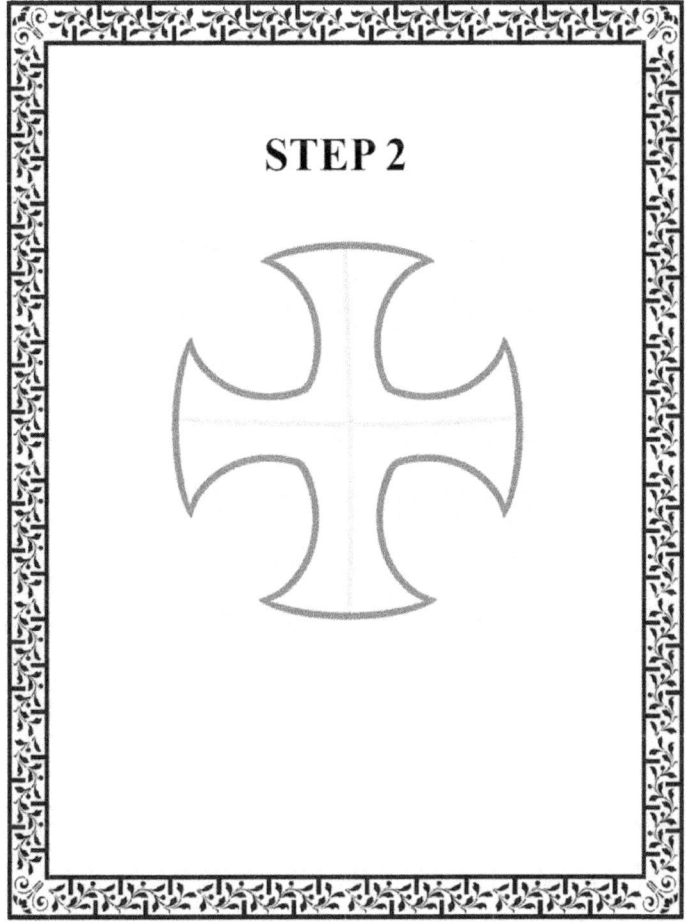

STEP 3

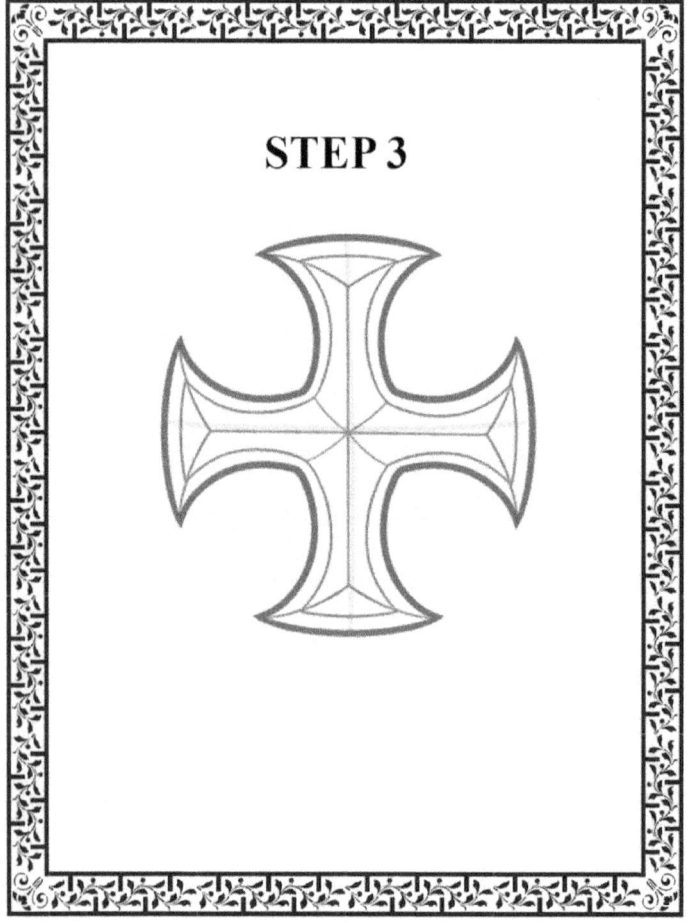

STEP 4

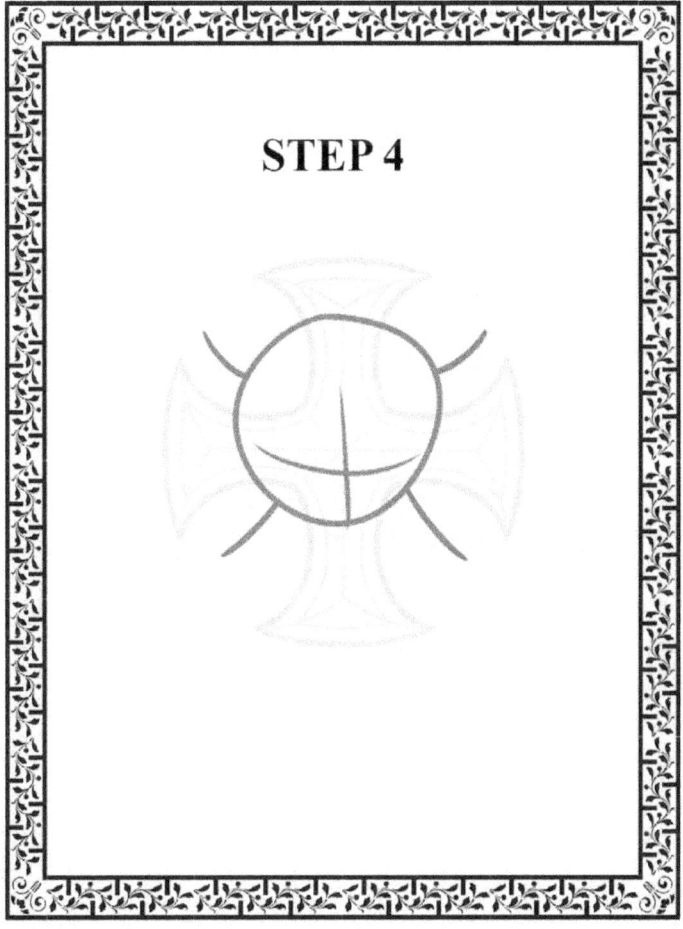

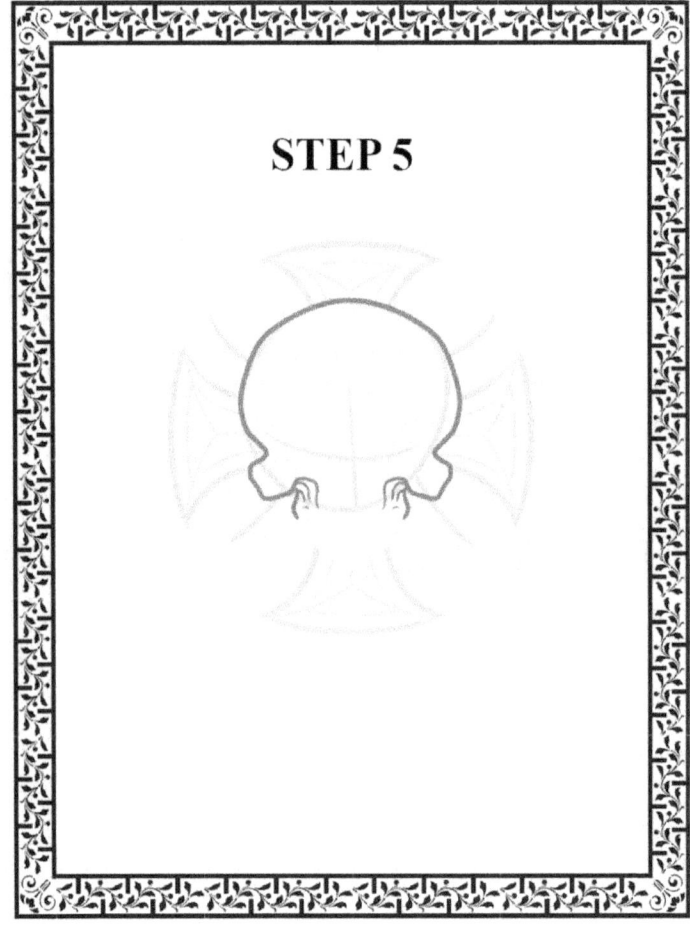

STEP 5

STEP 6

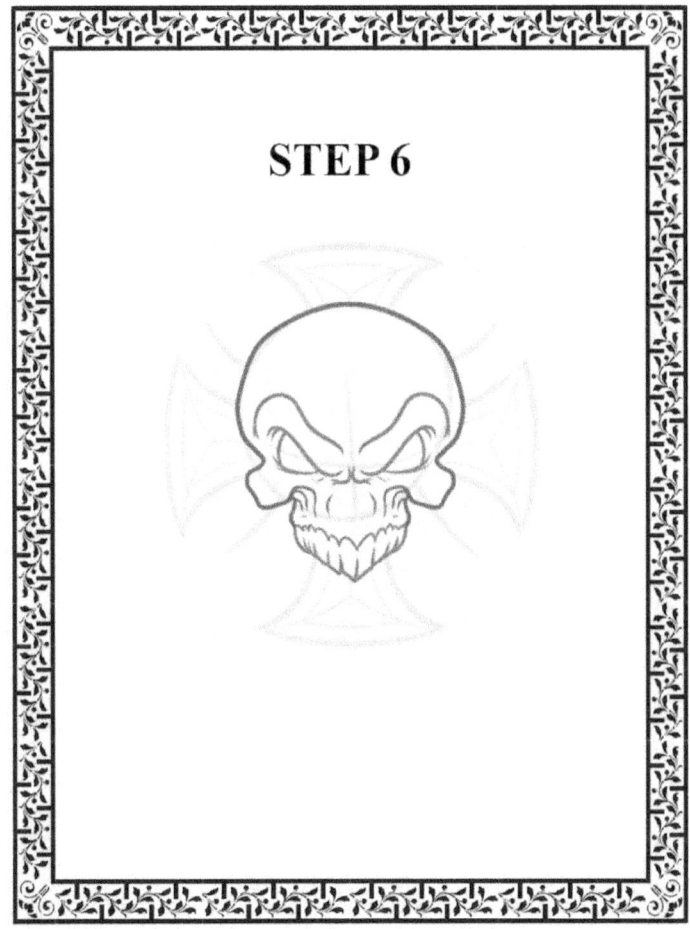

STEP 7

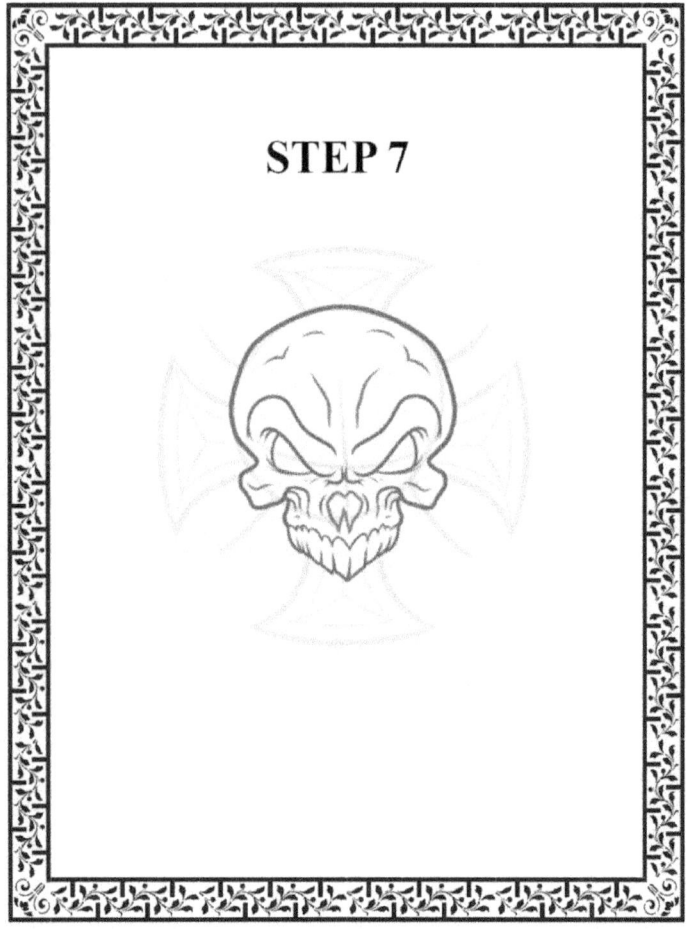

STEP 8

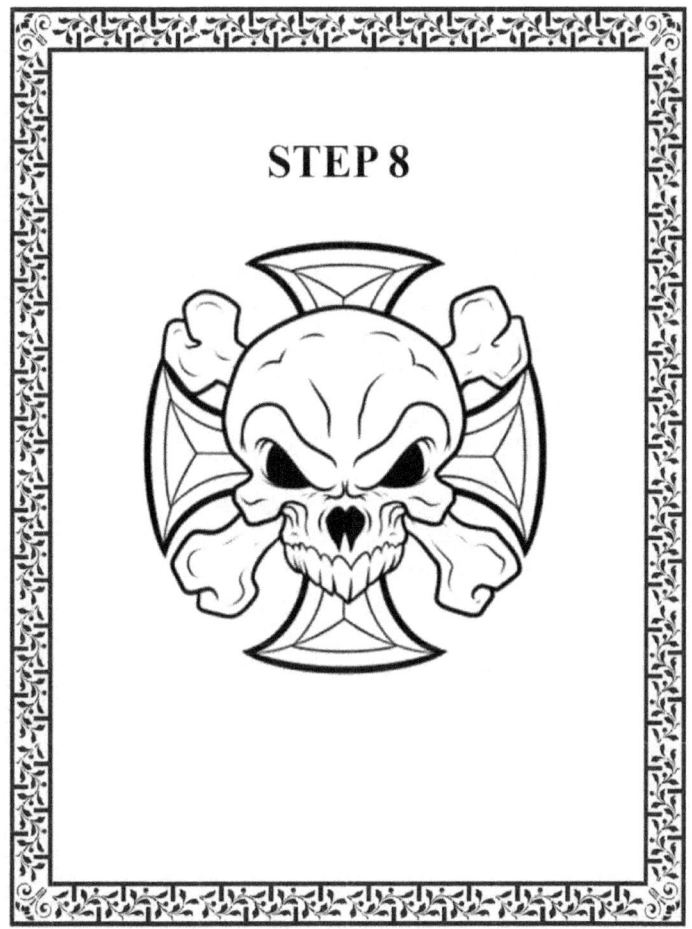

MOTH SKULL

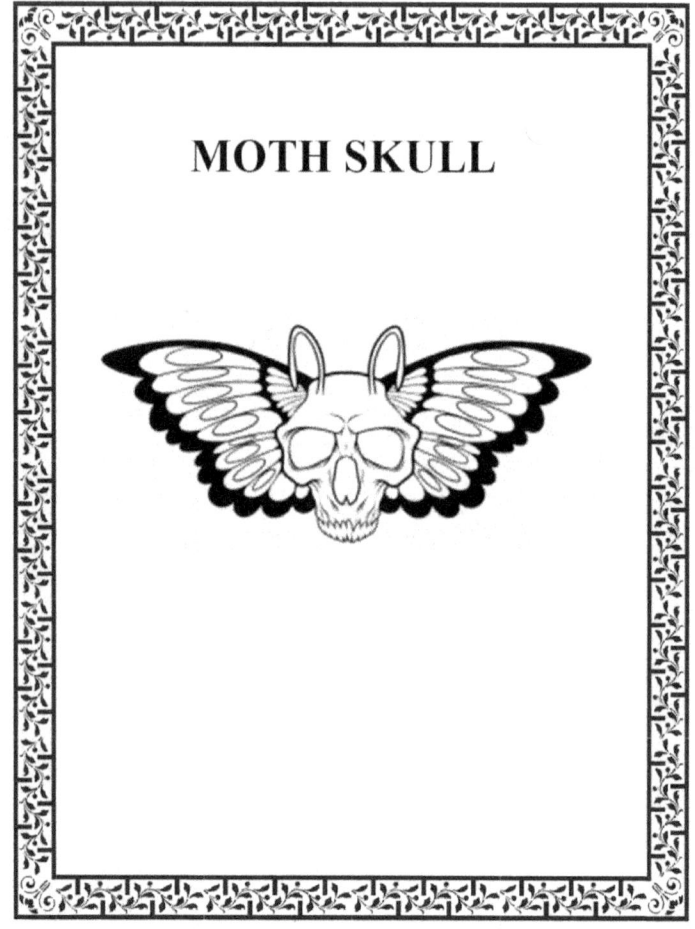

STEP 1

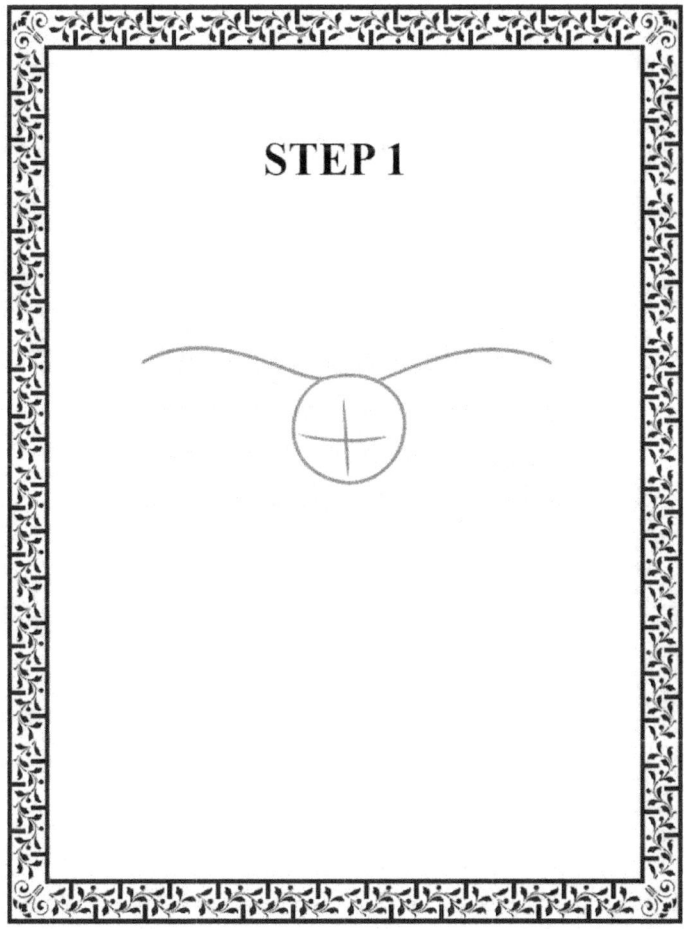

STEP 2

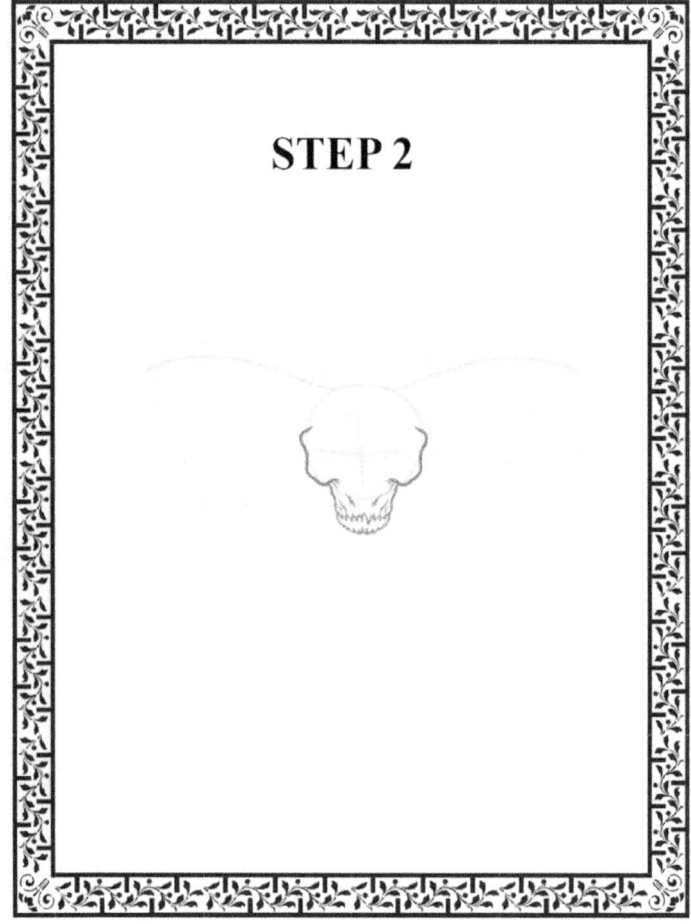

STEP 3

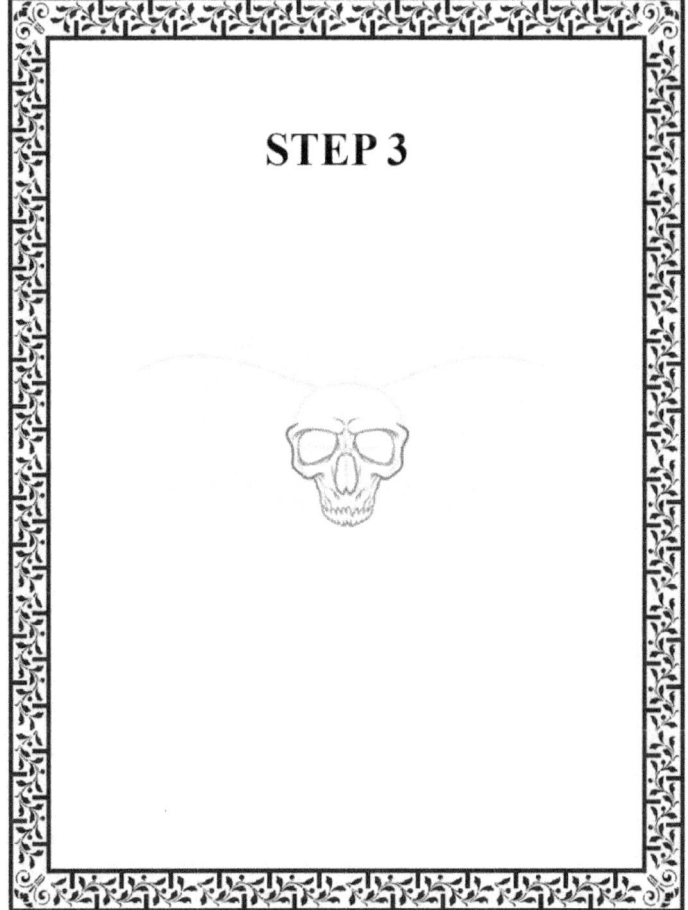

STEP 4

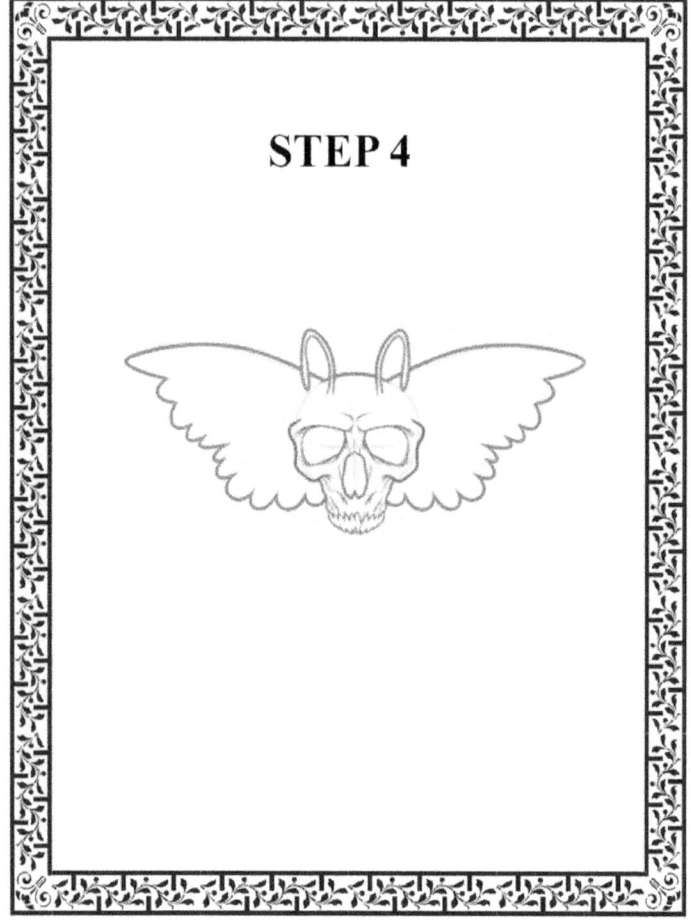

STEP 5

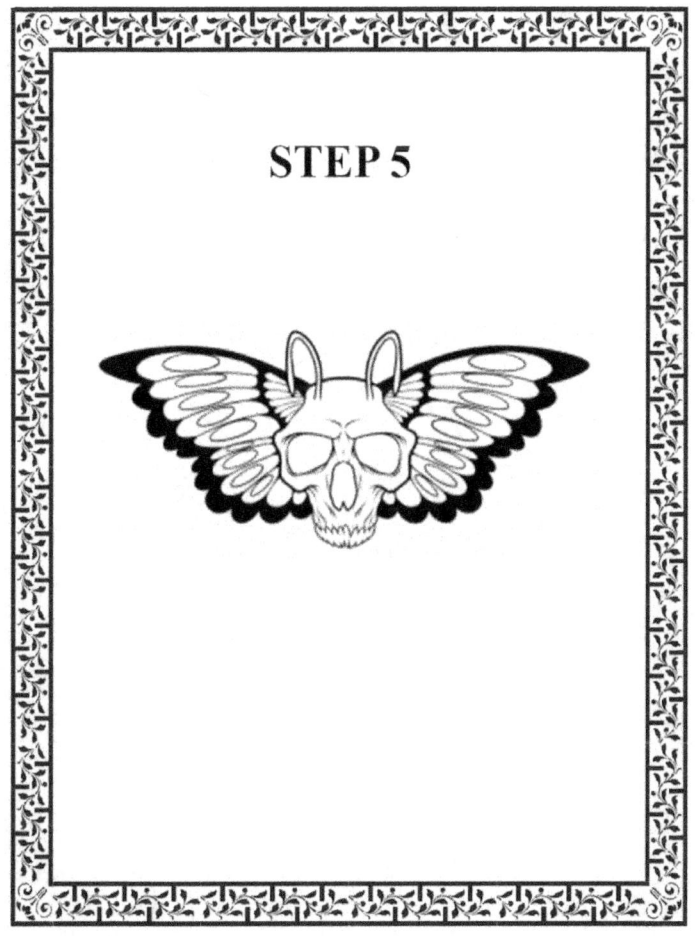

PIRATE SKULL

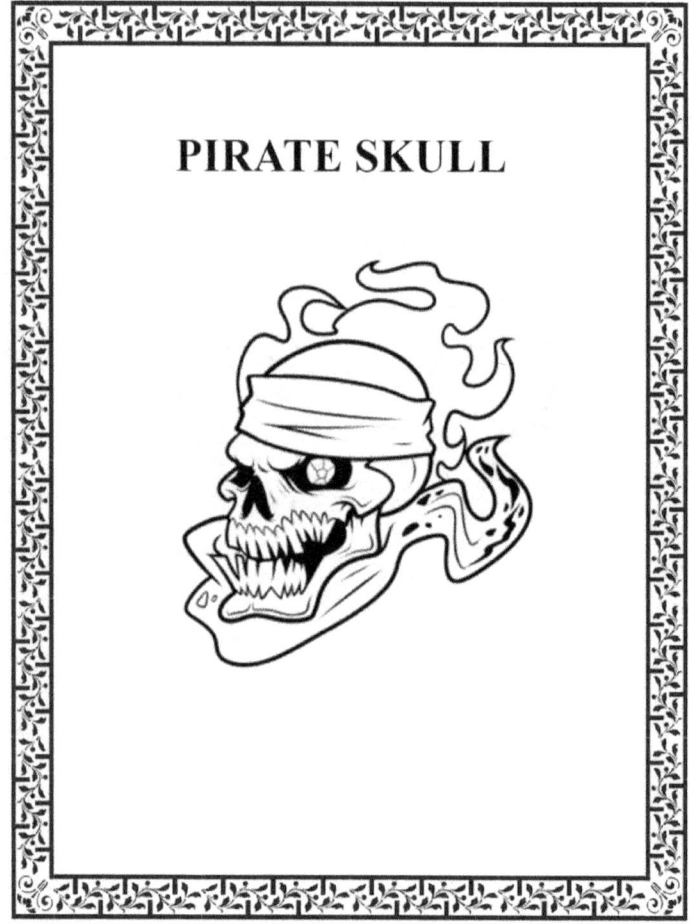

STEP 1

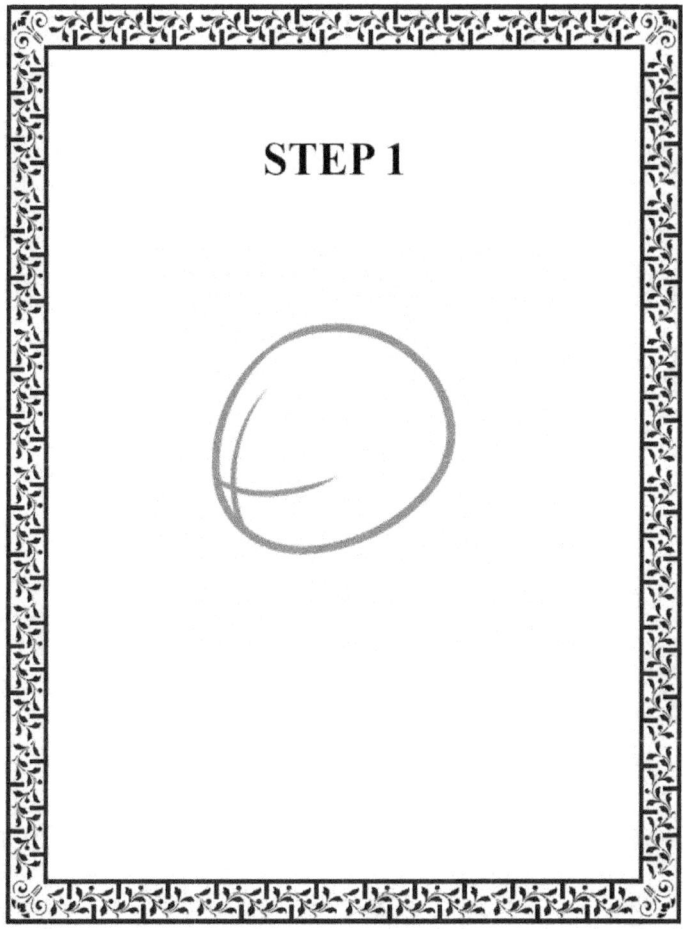

STEP 2

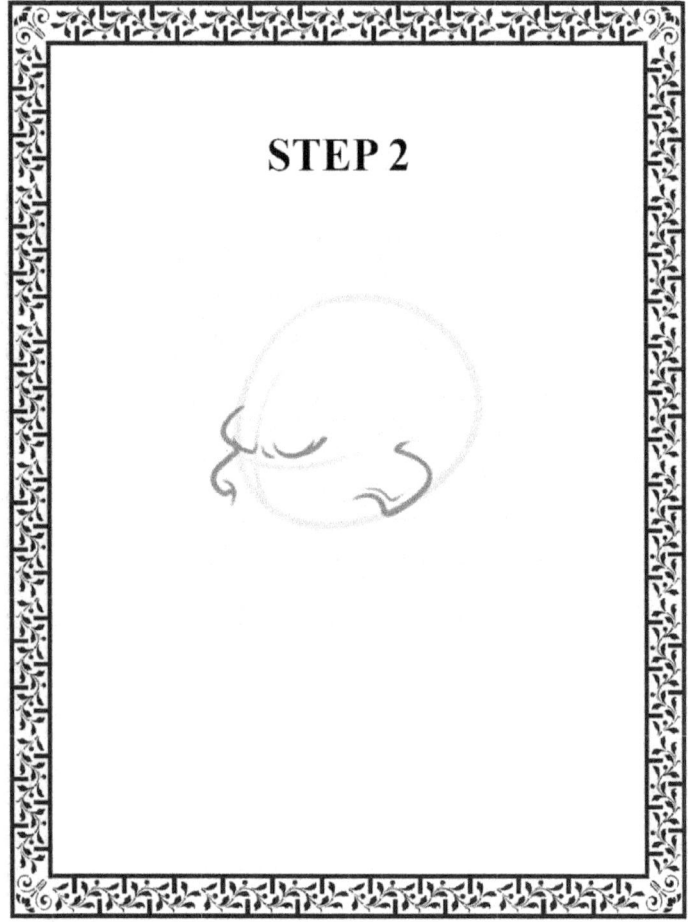

STEP 3

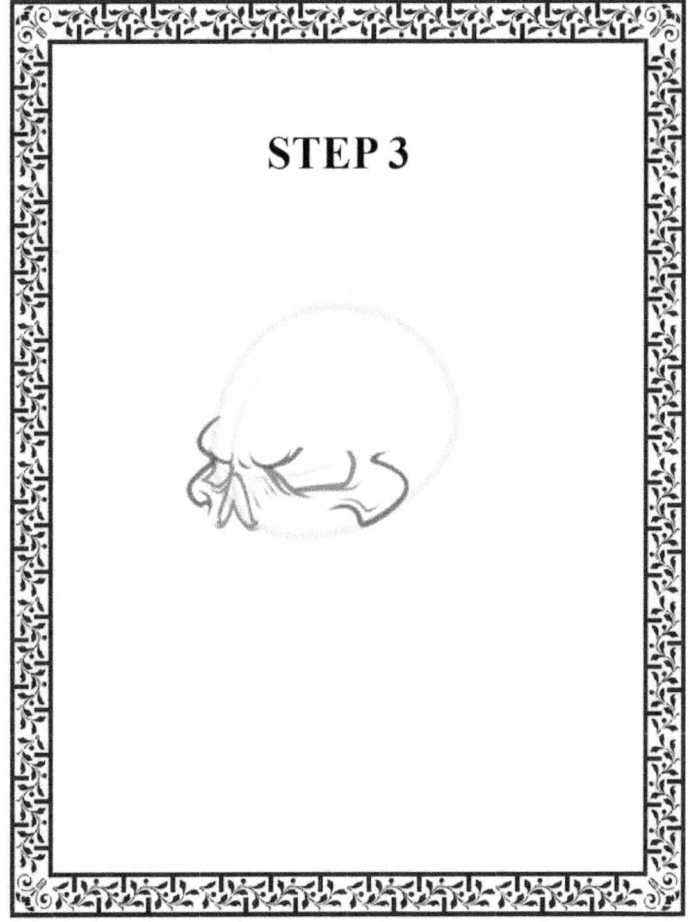

STEP 4

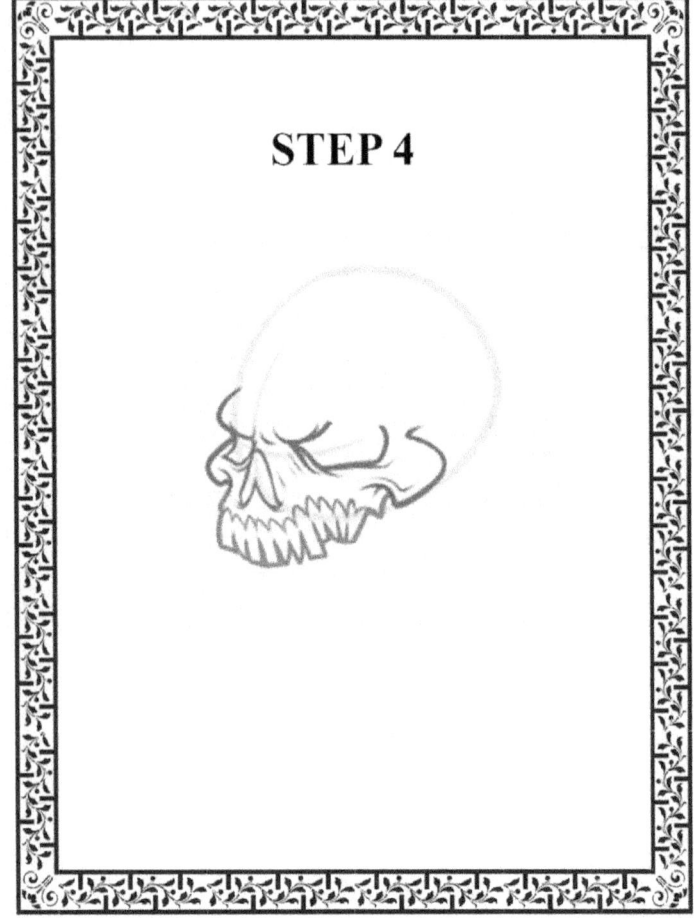

STEP 5

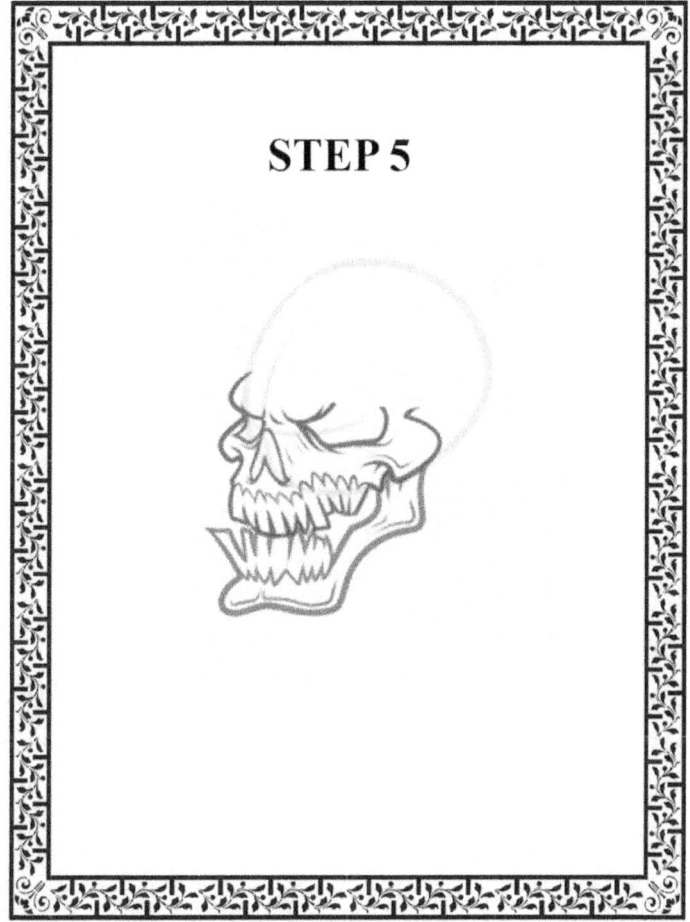

STEP 6

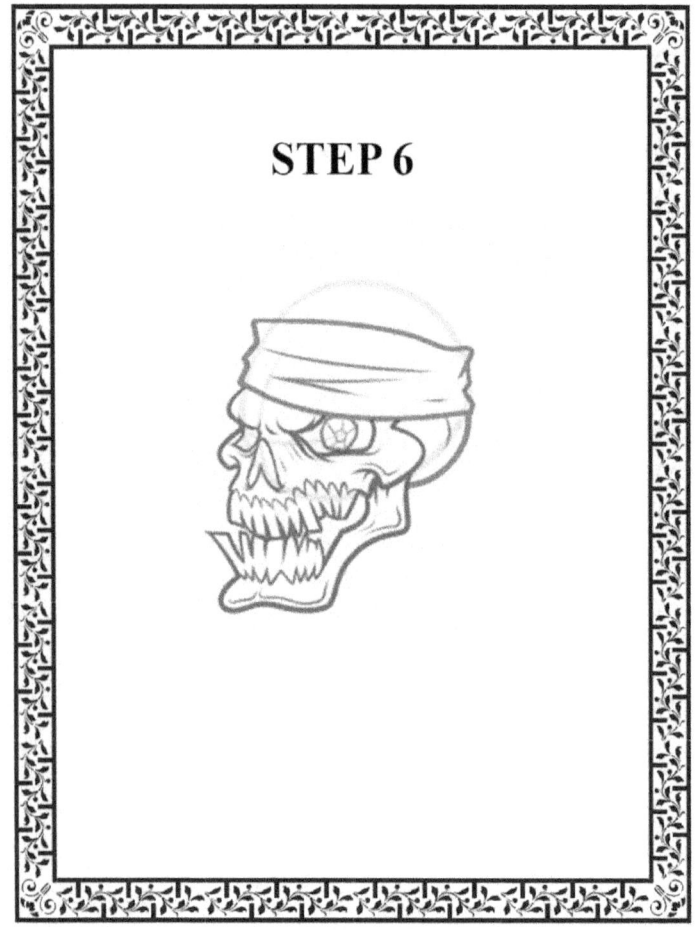

STEP 7

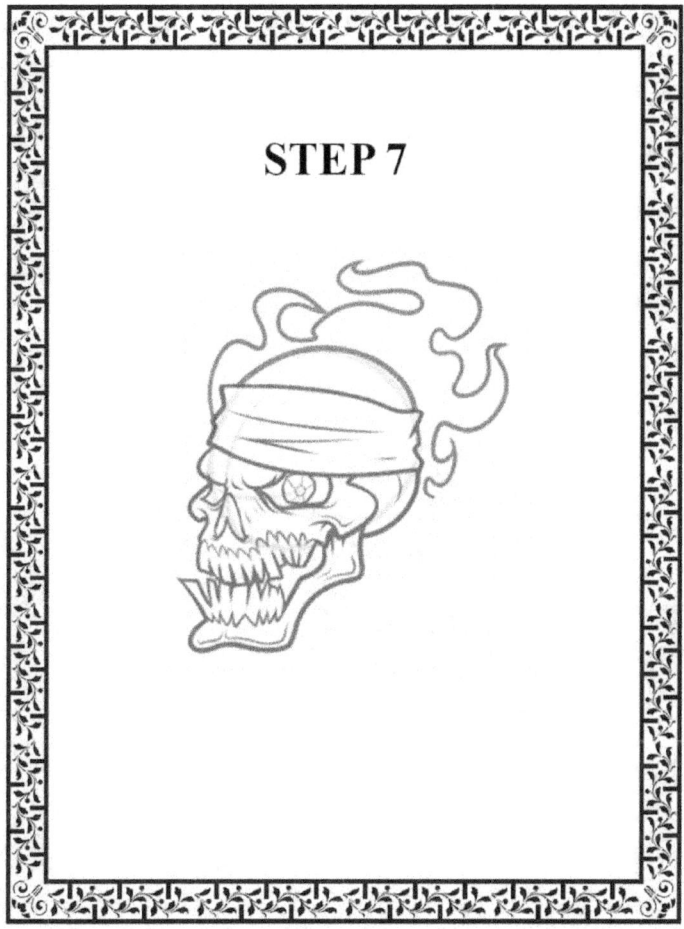

STEP 8

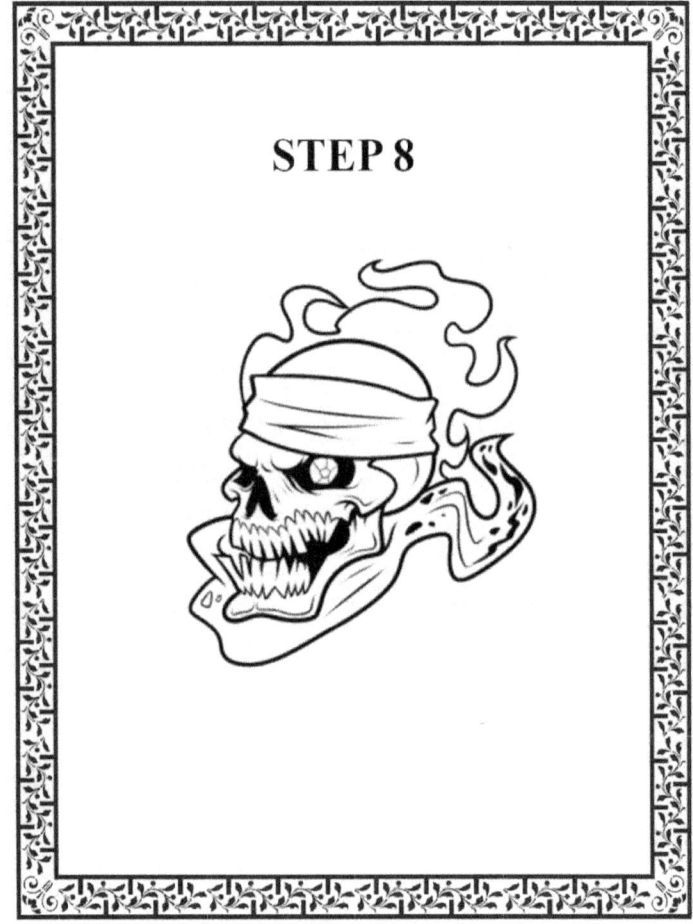

www.ingramcontent.com/pod-product-compliance
Lightning Source LLC
Chambersburg PA
CBHW071649170526
45166CB00003B/1494